How to Become the
Best Version of You?

A practical guide for Busy Leaders
to help improve your Health,
Wellbeing & Results

ANURAG RAI

AMHWAL Academy Ltd

www.amhwal.com

How To Become The Best Version Of You?

Copyright © 2024 AMHWAL Academy Ltd

AMHWAL Academy Ltd.
www.amhwal.com

Preface

Welcome to "How to Become the Best Version of You?" a journey not just of self-improvement but of self-discovery and transformation. This book is born from a simple yet profound realization that each of us has an immense potential waiting to be unleashed, a version of ourselves that is the fullest expression of our capabilities, dreams, and values.

The pursuit of becoming your best version is a universal one, transcending age, background, and circumstance. It's about aligning your actions with your deepest values, unlocking your latent talents, and transforming your dreams into reality. This journey is as unique as you are, and there is no one-size-fits-all approach.

In these pages, you'll find a guide that combines practical advice with reflective exercises. Each chapter addresses key areas of personal growth—from understanding your true self, setting meaningful goals, developing resilience, to enhancing emotional intelligence and beyond. These are not just topics; they are gateways to a deeper understanding of what you can achieve.

Embarking on this journey requires commitment—a willingness to confront your fears, challenge your existing beliefs, and step out of your comfort zone. It's a commitment that demands persistence and courage, but the rewards are immeasurable. You'll discover strengths you never knew you had, forge deeper relationships, and find a sense of purpose that lights up your life.

As you turn these pages, I invite you to engage actively with the content. Reflect on the questions posed, complete the exercises, and apply the lessons to your daily life. This is not just a book to be read; it's an experience to be lived.

Remember, becoming your best version isn't a destination; it's a continuous journey. There will be highs and lows, successes and setbacks, but every step forward brings you closer to the person you aspire to be. So, with an open heart and a curious mind, let's begin this journey together. The path to becoming your best version starts now.

Chapter 1: Discovering Yourself

The first step in becoming your best version is understanding who you are. This chapter guides you through the process of self-discovery, helping you identify your core values, strengths, weaknesses, passions, and emotional patterns.

Uncovering Your Core Values: Your values are the guiding principles of your life. Reflect on moments when you felt most fulfilled or proud—these are clues to your core values. Identify and list your top values, such as honesty, compassion, or ambition, and consider how they shape your decisions and actions.

Assessing Strengths and Weaknesses: Gaining insight into your strengths and weaknesses is crucial for personal growth. Utilize tools like SWOT (Strengths, Weaknesses, Opportunities, Threats) analysis to evaluate yourself. Embrace your strengths and acknowledge areas where you need improvement, setting the stage for targeted personal development.

Discovering Passions and Purpose: Identifying what truly drives you is key to defining your purpose. Think about activities that make you lose track of time or bring you joy. These passions often point towards your purpose, guiding your choices in life and career.

Emotional Self-Discovery: Develop emotional awareness by recognizing and understanding your emotions and their impact on your decisions. Practice identifying your emotions in different situations and explore their origins and influences.

The Power of Beliefs: Your beliefs shape your view of the world and your place in it. Reflect on the beliefs that guide your life. Are they empowering or limiting? Challenge limiting beliefs and work towards adopting beliefs that support your growth and goals.

Use the insights gained from this chapter as a foundation for your journey towards becoming your best version. Recognize that self-discovery is an ongoing process, with each step revealing more about your true self.

Suggested Exercises

1. **"My True North: Identifying Core Values"**

   Let's start by pinpointing what truly matters to you. Below is a list of values like integrity, creativity, and compassion. Select the five that resonate most deeply with you. Feel free to choose one that is not on the list. For each, reflect on why it's essential in your life and how you currently honour it. This isn't just an exercise; it's a journey to the heart of who you are, helping you make choices that deeply align with your inner self.

   - Integrity: Adhering to moral and ethical principles.
   - Compassion: Showing empathy and kindness to others.
   - Courage: Facing challenges and fears bravely.
   - Respect: Valuing and considering others' feelings and rights.
   - Loyalty: Being faithful and devoted to someone or something.
   - Creativity: Valuing innovative thinking and originality.
   - Ambition: Having a strong desire for success or achievement.
   - Generosity: Willingness to give and share unselfishly.
   - Wisdom: Possessing experience, knowledge, and good judgment.
   - Independence: Valuing self-reliance and autonomy.
   - Justice: Pursuing fairness and moral righteousness.
   - Humility: Having a modest view of one's own importance.

- Perseverance: Persisting steadfastly in spite of difficulties.
- Honesty: Being truthful and transparent.
- Responsibility: Being accountable for one's actions and duties.
- Empathy: Understanding and sharing the feelings of others.
- Gratitude: Appreciating and valuing what we have.
- Optimism: Having a hopeful and positive outlook on life.
- Balance: Maintaining a healthy equilibrium in life.
- Passion: Strong enthusiasm or excitement for something.

2. **"Mapping My World: Personal SWOT Analysis"**

Here's a tool you can use for self-reflection: SWOT Analysis, but with a personal twist. Consider your strengths and weaknesses, as well as opportunities for growth and potential obstacles. This can relate to any aspect of your life you're focusing on improving. By understanding these elements, you'll gain a clearer vision of where you stand and where you can go, setting the stage for meaningful personal development.

3. **"Emotional Exploration: A Week-Long Journal"**

For the next week, I invite you to embark on an emotional exploration. Whenever you experience a strong emotion, jot it down. Note the situation, your reaction, and ponder why you felt this way. This exercise goes beyond recognizing emotions; it's about understanding what triggers them and how you respond. It's a powerful tool for enhancing emotional intelligence, leading to better self-management and more empathetic relationships.

Each of these exercises is designed to offer you deeper insights into yourself. As you work through them, remember that personal growth is a continuous journey, and these tools are your companions along the way.

Chapter 2: Setting Personal Goals

The path to becoming your best version is paved with clear, purposeful goals. This chapter delves into the art and science of goal setting, empowering you to create a vision for your future and a roadmap to get there.

Understanding Goal Setting: Discover the different types of goals - short-term and long-term, personal, and professional. Embrace the SMART (Specific, Measurable, Achievable, Relevant, Time-bound) criteria, transforming broad aspirations into tangible objectives. Learn to distinguish between mere dreams and actionable goals, setting the foundation for real progress.

Setting Effective Goals: Begin by identifying what you truly want to achieve. Reflect on your values, passions, and strengths to align your goals with your personal vision. Break down larger goals into smaller, actionable steps and prioritize them. This step-by-step approach ensures manageability and keeps you motivated.

Overcoming Obstacles in Goal Setting: Address common challenges like fear of failure, procrastination, and setting unrealistic goals. Develop strategies to overcome these barriers, such as positive self-talk, time management techniques, and setting realistic expectations. Learn to maintain motivation by setting deadlines, tracking progress, and celebrating small victories.

The Power of Visualization: Enhance your goal-setting process with visualization techniques. Imagine yourself achieving your goals, experiencing the success, and overcoming obstacles. Create a vision board representing your goals, serving as a daily source of inspiration and a constant reminder of your objectives.

Incorporating Flexibility: Understand that flexibility is key in goal setting. Life's unpredictable nature means that your goals might need to be adjusted over time. Learn to embrace change and adapt your goals, accordingly, viewing each alteration not as a setback but as an evolution in your journey.

Goal Setting in Different Life Areas: Explore setting goals in various areas of life such as health, career, relationships, personal growth, and hobbies. Recognize that balanced goal setting across different life domains contributes to overall well-being and fulfilment.

Regularly review and reflect on your goals to track your progress and make necessary adjustments. Understand that goal setting is a dynamic and ongoing process, evolving as you grow and learn.

Suggested Exercises:

1. **"Crafting Our Vision: Building a Vision Board"**

Let's bring our dreams to life visually. Gather materials that resonate with your aspirations - this could be images from magazines, inspiring quotes, or anything that represents your goals. Create a collage on a board or digitally. Place it where you'll see it every day. This vision board will serve as a daily reminder of where we're headed, keeping us motivated and focused on our journey.

2. "The SMART Path: Goal Setting Worksheet"

Now, it's time to turn our dreams into achievable goals. I've prepared a worksheet based on the SMART criteria. Let's take one goal you're passionate about and break it down. What specific steps will it take? How will you measure progress? Is it achievable? Why is it relevant to you? What's the time frame? This process will transform your aspirations into tangible, actionable objectives, paving a clear path to success.

3. "Reflect, Adapt, Succeed: Monthly Goal Review"

Our journey is ever evolving, and so should our goals. I encourage you to dedicate time each month to reflect on your goals. Assess your progress, confront any challenges, and consider if your goals still align with your evolving self. This isn't just a review; it's an opportunity to adapt and refine, ensuring our goals remain aligned with our personal growth and changing circumstances.

These exercises are more than just tasks; they're stepping stones on our journey to becoming the best versions of ourselves. By actively engaging in these processes, we ensure that our goals are not only set but are also meaningful, dynamic, and aligned with our life's path.

Chapter 3: Cultivating a Growth Mindset

Embracing a growth mindset, a concept pioneered by psychologist Carol Dweck, is essential in the journey of self-improvement and reaching your full potential. This chapter delves into transforming your approach to challenges, learning, and failure, fostering a mindset that embraces growth and continuous learning.

Understanding Mindset: A growth mindset is about believing that your abilities and intelligence can be developed over time. Contrast this with a fixed mindset, where abilities are seen as static. Explore traits of a growth mindset such as embracing challenges, persisting in the face of setbacks, seeing effort as the path to mastery, learning from criticism, and finding lessons and inspiration in the success of others.

Developing a Growth Mindset: Learn strategies to nurture a growth mindset. Start by embracing challenges as opportunities to learn rather than threats to your intelligence or talent. Develop resilience and the ability to bounce back from setbacks or failures, viewing them as integral parts of the learning process.

Overcoming Limiting Beliefs: Identify and confront your own limiting beliefs that hinder growth. Practice challenging these beliefs and replace them with empowering growth-oriented ones. Understand the role of self-talk in nurturing a growth mindset and how to shift your internal narrative towards positivity and possibility.

Growth in Action: A growth mindset can be applied in real-life situations. It's about looking at situations and circumstances from a different lens, where you look for opportunities and possibilities. There are many stories and case studies of individuals who have exemplified a growth mindset in various aspects of life. Reflect on how to apply this mindset in your daily activities, from professional endeavours to personal hobbies and relationships.

Cultivating Lifelong Learning: A growth mindset goes hand in hand with lifelong learning. Explore ways to foster continuous learning in your life, whether through formal education, new experiences, or personal reading and research. Understand how embracing new challenges and stepping out of your comfort zone can significantly contribute to your personal growth.

Reflect on the importance of a growth mindset in your personal development journey. Recognize that cultivating this mindset is a continual process, one that enriches all aspects of your life and sets you up for long-term success and fulfilment.

Suggested Exercises:

Here are three exercises to help cultivate a growth mindset:

1. **Challenge Reflection Journal**

   - **Objective:** To reflect on challenges and learn from them.

   - **Description:** Keep a journal for a month. Each time you face a challenge, big or small, write it down. Detail what the challenge was, how you felt, how you reacted, and most importantly, what you learned from it.

   - **Outcome:** This exercise helps to reframe challenges as opportunities for growth, encouraging a mindset shift from avoidance to engagement and learning.

2. **The Effort Appreciation Diary**

   - **Objective:** To recognize and value the effort over success.

- **Description:** For two weeks, make a daily note of the efforts you put into various tasks, rather than focusing solely on the outcomes. Acknowledge and celebrate the effort itself, regardless of whether it led to success or failure.

- **Outcome:** This exercise aims to shift the focus from viewing success as a measure of intelligence or ability to seeing effort as the path to mastery and growth.

3. **Positive Self-Talk Practice**

- **Objective:** To develop a habit of positive and growth-oriented self-talk.

- **Description:** Whenever you catch yourself engaging in negative self-talk, especially in the face of setbacks, consciously reframe those thoughts. For example, replace "I can't do this" with "I can't do this yet, but I can learn with time and effort."

- **Outcome:** This exercise helps to build a more positive and resilient mindset, essential for embracing a growth mindset and overcoming challenges.

These exercises are designed to encourage a shift in perspective, recognizing challenges as opportunities, valuing effort, and fostering positive self-talk, all key aspects of developing a growth mindset.

Chapter 4: Building Effective Habits

In the quest to become your best version, the habits you cultivate play a pivotal role. This chapter focuses on understanding the power of habits, how to effectively build new ones, and transform your daily life through consistent, purposeful actions.

The Power of Habits: Habits are the small decisions and actions you perform daily. Over time, these behaviours become automatic, shaping your life's trajectory. They are the compound interest of self-improvement; tiny changes can lead to significant results over time. Understanding this can be a game-changer in how you approach personal development.

Understanding Habit Formation: The formation of habits is rooted in a simple but powerful pattern: the cue-routine-reward loop. A cue triggers a behaviour (routine), which is then followed by a reward. Recognizing this pattern in your existing habits is the first step in mastering new ones. By identifying your routines and what prompts and rewards them, you can begin to make intentional changes.

Identifying Current Habits: Start by assessing your current habits. Which of these contribute positively to your life, and which are holding you back? This self-awareness is crucial for setting the stage for change.

Creating New Habits: To build new habits, start small. Choose one habit you want to develop that aligns with your goals. Make it so easy that you can't say no. For instance, if you want to exercise more, start with five minutes a day, not an hour. Consistency is more important than intensity at the beginning.

The Role of Environment in Habit Formation: Your environment plays a significant role in habit formation. Make desired behaviours easy and convenient. If you want to read more, place books in visible, accessible places around your home. Conversely, make undesirable habits difficult to perform. If you're trying to eat healthier, don't stock junk food in your pantry.

Building Habit Streaks: Use Habit Streaks to build momentum. Mark each day you perform your new habit on a calendar. As the chain grows, you'll become more motivated to maintain it. This visual representation of your progress can be a powerful motivator.

Breaking Unhealthy Habits: To break a bad habit, make it visible, unattractive, difficult, and unsatisfying. If you're trying to reduce screen time, turn off notifications, or leave your phone in another room. Replace the negative habit with a positive one that provides a similar reward.

Dealing with Setbacks: Understand that setbacks are a normal part of habit formation. When you slip, it's not a failure; it's part of the process. The key is to get back on track as quickly as possible without self-judgment.

Sustaining Habits Long-Term: To sustain habits long-term, integrate them into your identity. Instead of just doing the habit, embody it. If you exercise regularly, consider yourself an athlete. This mindset shift is crucial for long-term adherence.

Tracking and Reviewing Habits: Tracking your habits provides valuable feedback. Use a habit tracker to monitor your progress and review it regularly. This can help you understand what's working, what isn't, and why.

Habit Stacking: Habit stacking involves linking a new habit to an existing one. After [current habit], I will [new habit]. For example, after brushing my teeth, I will meditate for one minute. This technique leverages your existing routines to incorporate new habits seamlessly.

Habit formation is a journey of self-discovery and improvement. By understanding the mechanics of habits, intentionally creating positive behaviours, and learning to navigate setbacks, you equip yourself with the tools for lasting change.

Suggested Exercises

Here are some exercises for building effective habits:

1. **Habit Audit Exercise:**

   - **Objective:** To identify and evaluate current habits.

   - **Description:** Create a habit inventory. For one week, track all your daily routines and habits. Categorize them into 'good' (positive impact), 'bad' (negative impact), and 'neutral' (no significant impact). For each habit, note the cue (trigger), routine (behaviour), and reward.

   - **Outcome:** This exercise helps you gain awareness of your existing habits, understand their triggers and rewards, and sets the stage for intentional change.

2. **Small Steps Habit Formation:**

   - **Objective:** To establish a new positive habit.

   - **Description:** Select one small habit you want to develop that aligns with your goals. Make it incredibly easy to start (e.g., if you want to start a reading habit, begin with reading one page every night). Do this for at least 21 consecutive days, gradually increasing the intensity as it becomes part of your routine.

- **Outcome:** This exercise emphasizes the power of small, consistent actions in building new habits, reducing the overwhelm of big changes.

3. **Environment Design for Habit Success:**

   - **Objective:** To modify your environment to support new habits.

   - **Description:** Identify environmental factors that can be altered to support your new habit. If your goal is to eat healthier, stock your fridge with healthy snacks and remove junk food. If you want to exercise in the morning, lay out your workout clothes the night before.

   - **Outcome:** By optimizing your environment, this exercise aims to reduce friction in practicing new habits and remove triggers for negative habits.

4. **Habit Stacking Technique:**

   - **Objective:** To incorporate a new habit into your existing routine.

   - **Description:** Choose a new habit and a current habit (a stable and consistent one). Formulate a plan: "After [current habit], I will [new habit]." For example, "After I brush my teeth, I will meditate for five minutes."

   - **Outcome:** This exercise leverages the power of existing routines to seamlessly integrate new habits, utilizing the consistency of established behaviours to trigger new ones.

Each of these exercises is designed to actively engage you in the process of understanding, creating, and maintaining habits. They offer a practical approach to modifying your daily routines and behaviours, crucial for personal growth and achieving your goals.

Chapter 5: Enhancing Emotional Intelligence

Emotional Intelligence (EI) is a key factor in achieving personal and professional success and fulfilment. This chapter delves into the facets of EI - understanding and managing your own emotions, empathizing with others, and navigating social complexities skilfully.

Understanding Emotional Intelligence: EI encompasses several core skills: self-awareness, self-regulation, motivation, empathy, and social skills. It's not just about controlling emotions but understanding and using them effectively. EI influences how we manage behaviour, navigate social complexities, and make personal decisions that achieve positive results.

Developing Self-Awareness: Self-awareness is the foundation of EI. It's about recognizing and understanding your own emotions and how they affect your thoughts and actions. This involves being mindful of your emotional state and its impact, not only on yourself but on others around you. To enhance self-awareness, start by regularly checking in with your emotions and naming them. Understanding your emotional triggers can help you respond more effectively in different situations.

Mastering Self-Regulation: Self-regulation involves managing your emotions, particularly in stressful or challenging situations. It's about expressing your emotions appropriately and not letting them overpower your values or rational thinking. Techniques like deep breathing, mindfulness, and pausing before reacting are vital in developing this skill. By managing your emotional reactions, you can make more reasoned decisions and respond more constructively in difficult situations.

Cultivating Intrinsic Motivation: Intrinsic motivation is about being driven by internal rewards, such as personal growth, a sense of achievement, or the pursuit of a passion, rather than external factors like money or status. To strengthen this aspect of EI, set goals that align with your personal values and interests. Reflect on what activities make you feel most alive and engaged and find ways to integrate them into your daily life.

Developing Empathy: Empathy is the ability to understand and share the feelings of others. It's a critical component of building strong, healthy relationships. To develop empathy, practice active listening and try to see situations from others' perspectives. This not only helps in personal relationships but also in professional settings, where understanding diverse viewpoints is crucial.

Enhancing Social Skills: Effective social skills are vital for building and maintaining relationships. This includes skills like clear communication, conflict resolution, and the ability to influence others positively. To improve these skills, focus on understanding social cues and responding appropriately. Engage in activities that require team collaboration, and practice different communication styles and techniques.

Emotional Intelligence in Relationships: EI plays a significant role in forming and maintaining healthy relationships. It involves understanding your emotions and those of others and navigating interactions sensitively and effectively. Practice empathy and active listening in your relationships and focus on building mutual understanding and respect.

Emotional Intelligence in the Workplace: In a professional context, EI is crucial for leadership, teamwork, and overall workplace harmony. Leaders with high EI can inspire and motivate their teams more effectively. Focus on developing EI skills like empathy, social awareness, and conflict resolution to enhance your professional relationships and leadership abilities.

Developing EI is a lifelong journey that can lead to more fulfilling personal and professional relationships, better mental health, and overall well-being. By enhancing your EI, you equip yourself with the tools to navigate life's challenges more effectively and build strong, meaningful connections with others.

EI Development Exercises

1. Self-Awareness Exercise: Emotion Logging

- **Description:** Keep an emotion log for a week. Throughout each day, note down your emotions at different times, what triggered them, and how you responded.

- **Purpose:** This exercise helps in recognizing patterns in emotional responses and understanding triggers, enhancing self-awareness.

2. Self-Regulation Exercise: The Pause Technique

- **Description:** When faced with a challenging situation, practice pausing before reacting. Count to 10, breathe deeply, and then respond.

- **Purpose:** This technique teaches how to manage impulsive reactions, allowing for more thoughtful and controlled responses.

3. Motivation Exercise: Visualizing Success

- **Description:** Spend a few minutes each day visualizing achieving a personal goal. Picture the steps involved, the challenges, and the final successful outcome.

- **Purpose:** This visualization technique boosts intrinsic motivation by keeping the end goal vivid and inspiring.

4. Empathy Exercise: Active Listening Practice

- **Description:** In conversations, focus entirely on the speaker. Listen without interrupting, and then repeat back what you understood to confirm accuracy.

- **Purpose:** Active listening enhances understanding of others' perspectives and feelings, fostering deeper empathy.

5. Social Skills Exercise: Relationship Building

- **Description:** Reach out to a colleague, friend, or family member and initiate a conversation about a topic of mutual interest. Focus on maintaining a balance between talking and listening.

- **Purpose:** This exercise helps in building stronger social connections and improving communication skills.

6. Conflict Resolution Exercise: Role-Reversal

- **Description:** In a conflict situation, try to articulate the other person's point of view and feelings before presenting your own.

- **Purpose:** Understanding and articulating the other person's perspective can lead to more effective conflict resolution and improved relationships.

These exercises are designed to be practical and applicable in everyday life, helping individuals to enhance their emotional intelligence in a structured and effective way.

Some Journal Prompts

Here are three journal prompts that can facilitate deeper reflection and enhance emotional intelligence:

1. **Exploring Emotional Patterns:**

   - **Prompt:** "Reflect on a recent situation where you experienced strong emotions. Describe the situation, the emotions you felt, and how you reacted. What might these feelings reveal about your values, fears, or unresolved issues? How could you handle similar situations more effectively in the future?"

2. **Understanding Others' Perspectives:**

   - **Prompt:** "Think about a recent interaction you had that was challenging or uncomfortable. Write about the experience from the other person's perspective. What might they have been feeling or thinking? How does this exercise change your understanding of the situation and your response to it?"

3. **Personal Growth and EI Goals:**

- **Prompt:** "What are three specific areas of emotional intelligence you want to develop (e.g., empathy, self-regulation, motivation)? For each area, write down why it's important to you and outline a plan of action for how you can improve in these areas over the next month."

These prompts are designed to encourage introspection and self-awareness, helping individuals to better understand their emotional responses, develop empathy, and set concrete goals for their emotional intelligence growth.

Chapter 6: Nutrition and Well-being

In the pursuit of becoming the best version of yourself, one of the cornerstones is a holistic approach to health and wellbeing. Nutrition plays a pivotal role in shaping not only your physical health but also your mental and emotional state. This chapter explores the profound impact of nutrition on your overall wellbeing and offers practical insights into cultivating a balanced and nourishing diet.

Understanding Nutritional Basics:

To embark on the journey of optimal wellbeing, it is essential to grasp the fundamentals of nutrition. Our bodies require a diverse range of nutrients, including carbohydrates, proteins, fats, vitamins, and minerals. These nutrients serve as the building blocks for energy production, immune function, and the maintenance of various bodily functions.

Creating a Balanced Plate:

Achieving the best version of yourself starts with what you put on your plate. Aim for a balanced and colorful mix of fruits, vegetables, lean proteins, whole grains, and healthy fats. Incorporate a variety of foods to ensure you receive a broad spectrum of nutrients. Pay attention to portion sizes to avoid overconsumption and maintain a healthy weight.

The Impact of Hydration:

Often overlooked, hydration is a fundamental aspect of nutrition. Water is essential for digestion, nutrient absorption, and the elimination of toxins from the body. Aim to drink an adequate amount of water throughout the day, and consider incorporating hydrating foods like fruits and vegetables into your diet.

Mindful Eating:

Cultivating a healthy relationship with food goes beyond what you eat—it involves how you eat. Practicing mindful eating encourages you to savour each bite, be aware of your hunger and fullness cues, and appreciate the nourishment your food provides. This approach can enhance digestion, reduce overeating, and foster a deeper connection with your body.

Navigating Nutritional Challenges:

In the modern world, where processed and convenience foods abound, making healthy choices can be challenging. Learn to read food labels, minimize the intake of sugary and highly processed foods, and prioritize whole, nutrient-dense options. Consider consulting with a registered dietitian for personalized guidance tailored to your individual needs and goals.

Fuelling Physical and Mental Performance:

Your nutritional choices have a direct impact on your physical and mental performance. Incorporate foods that support sustained energy levels, focus, and emotional wellbeing. Experiment with the timing and composition of your meals to discover what works best for you, whether you're an athlete striving for peak performance or someone looking to enhance cognitive function.

Nutrition is a cornerstone of your journey to becoming the best version of yourself. By embracing a balanced and mindful approach to eating, you provide your body and mind with the essential nutrients they need to thrive. Remember, the path to optimal wellbeing is unique for each individual, so take the time to discover what nourishes and energizes you, setting the stage for a healthier, more vibrant life.

Chapter 7: Lifelong Learning and Skill Development

In our pursuit of becoming our best selves, embracing lifelong learning and skill development is essential. This chapter is dedicated to understanding the importance of continuous learning.

The Essence of Lifelong Learning: Lifelong learning is about more than acquiring knowledge; it's a mindset of continuous personal and professional development. It involves staying curious, seeking new challenges, and always pushing our boundaries. This approach keeps our minds active, adaptable, and prepared for the ever-changing landscape of life.

Identifying Learning Opportunities: First, let's identify areas for growth. What skills or knowledge would enhance your life or career? Learning can take many forms, from formal education like online courses or workshops to informal activities such as reading, traveling, or exploring new hobbies. The key is to align your learning with your passions and goals.

Setting Learning Goals: Now, let's set some learning goals. Make them specific, measurable, achievable, relevant, and time bound. Break down each goal into smaller steps and create a timeline for achieving them. This structured approach makes your learning journey more manageable and less overwhelming.

Navigating Learning Challenges: Common challenges in learning include time constraints, financial limitations, or fear of failure. Tackle these by exploring alternative, often free, learning resources like MOOCs, podcasts, or community classes. Manage your time effectively by setting aside dedicated learning periods in your schedule.

Skill Acquisition Process: Acquiring a new skill is a rewarding process. Start small and practice consistently. Remember, proficiency comes with time and patience. Embrace the initial phase of learning with an open mind, and don't be discouraged by early challenges. Regular practice and gradual increase in complexity will lead to mastery.

Leveraging Technology for Learning: Technology offers an abundance of learning resources. Utilize online platforms for courses, educational apps for skill development, and digital tools for organizing and tracking your learning progress. These resources make learning accessible and flexible, fitting into your lifestyle.

Community and Collaborative Learning: Learning alongside others can be incredibly enriching. Engage in study groups, find mentors, or join online communities related to your learning interests. Sharing knowledge and experiences with others not only enhances your learning but also builds your network.

Maintaining Curiosity: Keep the flame of curiosity alive. Regularly challenge yourself with new questions and seek out answers. Stay open to new ideas and perspectives, as they can lead to unexpected and rewarding learning paths.

Embracing lifelong learning is a journey that enriches both your personal and professional life. It's about growing, adapting, and finding joy in continuous discovery. Keep learning, keep growing, and you'll find yourself moving ever closer to your best version.

Exercises for Lifelong Learning:

Here are three exercises that align with Chapter 7 on Lifelong Learning and Skill Development:

1. **Learning Pathway Mapping:**

- **Objective:** To identify and plan your personal learning journey.

- **Description:** Create a map or chart that outlines your learning goals. Start by listing areas you are curious about or skills you wish to develop. For each area or skill, break down the steps needed to achieve mastery. Include resources you can use, such as books, courses, workshops, or mentors. Set realistic timelines for each step.

- **Outcome:** This exercise helps in creating a clear and structured plan for your learning journey, making your goals more tangible and achievable.

2. **Skill Practice Schedule:**

- **Objective:** To develop a consistent practice routine for a new skill.

- **Description:** Choose a skill you want to learn or improve. Create a weekly schedule that allocates specific times for practicing this skill. During these practice sessions, focus solely on developing the skill, free from other distractions. Adjust the schedule as needed based on your progress and other commitments.

- **Outcome:** This exercise encourages the formation of a regular practice habit, essential for skill acquisition and improvement.

3. **Curiosity Journal:**

- **Objective:** To cultivate curiosity and open-mindedness.

- **Description:** Keep a journal for at least a month where you record anything that sparks your curiosity each day. It could be a topic, a question, a skill, or an idea. Each week, choose one item from your journal to explore further through research, experimentation, or discussion with others.

- **Outcome:** This exercise helps in nurturing a habit of curiosity, leading to a broader range of interests and a deeper engagement in continuous learning.

These exercises are designed to actively engage you in the process of lifelong learning, encouraging the development of a structured approach to acquiring new knowledge and skills while fostering curiosity and open-mindedness.

Chapter 8: Social Connections and Community

The journey to personal growth is deeply intertwined with our social connections and community involvement. This chapter emphasizes the importance of nurturing relationships and engaging with your community as vital elements of self-improvement.

The Role of Social Connections: Human connections are essential to our mental and emotional well-being. Strong relationships contribute to improved mental health, greater happiness, and even a longer life. Understanding the dynamics of these relationships is crucial in providing support, introducing new perspectives, and enriching life experiences.

Building and Maintaining Relationships: Key to fostering meaningful relationships are effective communication, empathy, and active listening. Strategies for strengthening existing relationships and building new ones include understanding others' viewpoints, expressing yourself clearly, and maintaining a balance of give and take.

Community Involvement: Participating in community activities provides a sense of belonging and purpose. Explore local volunteering opportunities, community events, or clubs that align with your interests. This engagement benefits personal growth and strengthens community bonds.

Professional Networking: Networking is invaluable in professional development. It involves creating sustainable professional relationships, understanding the value of mentorship, and utilizing social media platforms effectively. Each interaction is an opportunity for new learning and growth.

Overcoming Social Challenges: Addressing social challenges such as anxiety or conflict in relationships is part of personal development. Strategies to navigate these challenges include developing self-awareness, enhancing emotional intelligence, and applying conflict resolution skills.

Digital and Personal Interaction Balance: In an era dominated by digital communication, it's important to balance online interactions with face-to-face connections. Utilize technology effectively for maintaining relationships while also valuing the unique benefits of in-person interactions.

Empathy and Understanding: Empathy, the ability to understand and share the feelings of others, is crucial in building strong connections. Enhance empathy in both personal and professional relationships through active listening and trying to understand various perspectives.

Fostering social connections and actively participating in community life are integral to personal development. By engaging in the practices outlined in this chapter, you enhance your social well-being and contribute meaningfully to your journey of growth and self-improvement.

Actionable Steps:

1. **Relationship Mapping:** Identify key relationships in your life and set specific actions to strengthen these connections.

2. **Commit to Community Involvement:** Choose a local group or cause to engage with regularly. Reflect on how this involvement contributes to your growth.

3. **Professional Networking Goals:** Set clear objectives for expanding your professional network through events, associations, or informational interviews.

4. **Daily Empathy Practice:** In your daily interactions, focus on active listening and understanding the other person's perspective.

Chapter 8: Social Connections and Community

The journey to personal growth is deeply intertwined with our social connections and community involvement. This chapter emphasizes the importance of nurturing relationships and engaging with your community as vital elements of self-improvement.

The Role of Social Connections: Human connections are essential to our mental and emotional well-being. Strong relationships contribute to improved mental health, greater happiness, and even a longer life. Understanding the dynamics of these relationships is crucial in providing support, introducing new perspectives, and enriching life experiences.

Building and Maintaining Relationships: Key to fostering meaningful relationships are effective communication, empathy, and active listening. Strategies for strengthening existing relationships and building new ones include understanding others' viewpoints, expressing yourself clearly, and maintaining a balance of give and take.

Community Involvement: Participating in community activities provides a sense of belonging and purpose. Explore local volunteering opportunities, community events, or clubs that align with your interests. This engagement benefits personal growth and strengthens community bonds.

Professional Networking: Networking is invaluable in professional development. It involves creating sustainable professional relationships, understanding the value of mentorship, and utilizing social media platforms effectively. Each interaction is an opportunity for new learning and growth.

Overcoming Social Challenges: Addressing social challenges such as anxiety or conflict in relationships is part of personal development. Strategies to navigate these challenges include developing self-awareness, enhancing emotional intelligence, and applying conflict resolution skills.

Digital and Personal Interaction Balance: In an era dominated by digital communication, it's important to balance online interactions with face-to-face connections. Utilize technology effectively for maintaining relationships while also valuing the unique benefits of in-person interactions.

Empathy and Understanding: Empathy, the ability to understand and share the feelings of others, is crucial in building strong connections. Enhance empathy in both personal and professional relationships through active listening and trying to understand various perspectives.

Actionable Steps:

1. **Relationship Mapping:** Identify key relationships in your life and set specific actions to strengthen these connections.

2. **Commit to Community Involvement:** Choose a local group or cause to engage with regularly. Reflect on how this involvement contributes to your growth.

3. **Professional Networking Goals:** Set clear objectives for expanding your professional network through events, associations, or informational interviews.

4. **Daily Empathy Practice:** In your daily interactions, focus on active listening and understanding the other person's perspective.

Fostering social connections and actively participating in community life are integral to personal development. By engaging in the practices outlined in this chapter, you enhance your social well-being and contribute meaningfully to your journey of growth and self-improvement.

Chapter 9: Reflection and Continual Improvement

Embarking on the journey of self-improvement is a continuous process, where reflection and continual improvement are essential. This chapter is dedicated to cultivating these practices, enabling you to stay on track with your personal development goals.

The Power of Reflection: Reflection allows us to gain deeper insights into our behaviours, thoughts, and experiences.

Action Step -> *Set aside a weekly reflection session. During this time, review your actions and decisions from the past week, assess their alignment with your goals, and identify areas for improvement.*

Learning from Every Experience: Every experience, be it success or a setback, is a learning opportunity.

Action Step -> *After any significant event, take time to write down what happened, how you responded, and what you learned. This practice helps in transforming experiences into valuable lessons.*

Goal Setting for Future Growth: Setting and updating goals is crucial as you grow and evolve.

Action Step -> *Regularly review and update your goals. Every month, assess your progress and adjust your goals to reflect your current priorities and learning.*

Embracing and Adapting to Change: Change is constant and adapting to it is key to personal growth.

Action Step -> Reflect on recent changes in your life. Identify the skills or adjustments needed to adapt effectively and integrate these into your development plan.

Staying Motivated Over Time: Keeping yourself motivated is essential for long-term growth.

Action Step -> Create a 'motivation board' where you post your achievements, positive feedback, and inspirational quotes. This visual reminder will help maintain your motivation.

The Importance of a Growth Mindset: Maintaining a growth mindset is crucial for ongoing development.

Action Step -> Whenever you face a challenge, consciously remind yourself that it's an opportunity to learn. Jot down what this challenge teaches you about yourself and your capabilities.

Utilizing Feedback Effectively: Feedback is crucial for improvement.

Action Step -> Actively seek feedback from peers, mentors, or supervisors. Reflect on this feedback and make a plan to incorporate this into your personal growth strategy.

Continual improvement and reflection are ongoing processes that are integral to personal development. Keeping engaged with these practices ensures that you are always moving forward on your journey to become your best version.

Chapter 10 Conclusion: Embracing the Journey of Self-Improvement

As we close this chapter and indeed this journey through the various facets of personal growth, it's important to reflect on the overarching theme that has guided us: the pursuit of becoming our best version is a continuous, evolving journey, not a final destination.

Throughout this book, we've explored various dimensions of self-improvement, from the intricacies of emotional intelligence and the importance of physical well-being to the power of social connections and the value of lifelong learning. Each chapter has not only provided insights but also actionable steps to integrate these elements into your life.

Remember, the path to self-improvement is unique for each individual. It's about finding your rhythm, understanding what works best for you, and being patient with yourself as you navigate through the ups and downs of this journey. The steps and strategies outlined in each chapter are not prescriptive but rather a guide to help you carve out your path.

One key takeaway is the importance of balance - balancing work and play, challenge and relaxation, giving and receiving. In your pursuit of goals, don't lose sight of the small joys and moments of tranquillity that daily life offers. The journey is as much about the destinations you're striving for as it is about the experiences and learnings along the way.

As you continue on your journey, remember to regularly pause and reflect on your growth. Celebrate your achievements, no matter how small they may seem, and learn from the setbacks without being too hard on yourself. Each step, each decision, each challenge overcome is a part of your growth narrative.

The journey of self-improvement is not a solitary one. Seek support when needed, offer support when you can, and cherish the relationships that nurture and inspire you. Your growth influences those around you, just as they influence yours.

Embracing the Future: As you turn the page on this chapter, be excited about the future and the endless possibilities it holds. Armed with the tools, knowledge, and insights from this book, step forward with confidence and a willingness to embrace whatever comes your way. The journey to becoming your best self is ongoing, and each day brings new opportunities to grow, learn, and improve.

Thank you for joining me on this journey. May you continue to thrive, evolve, and shine as you journey towards becoming the very best version of yourself.

Anurag Rai
EXECUTIVE COACH, BEST SELLING AUTHOR, & ORGANISATIONAL PSYCHOLOGIST

anurag@amhwal.com

AMHWAL Academy is one of the leading training providers in Scotland for Mental Health, Wellbeing and Leadership Development. Our training is fun, practical, and transformational. Pieces of training combine the elements of neuroscience, psychology, and executive coaching to enable and empower trainees to change behaviours and personalities.

Our training programs are regularly updated to include the latest research in the fields of mental health, leadership, and human psychology. Our mission is to make corporate training more transformational and less educational.

AMHWAL Academy have experience of working with small, medium, and large organisations in the public and private sectors. Get in touch today to find out how we can help you in growing your people and organisation.

AMHWAL Academy Ltd

7 Queens Gardens, Aberdeen AB15 4YD

01224 619242 | info@amhwal.com